The Voice of Sleepless Nights

Bohdan Levko

BookLeaf Publishing

Presentation by *BookLeaf Publishing*

Web: www.bookleafpub.com

E-mail: info@bookleafpub.com

ISBN: 9789357614139

First edition 2022

To my family, which keeps supporting me through all the life choices I make.

Lost In a Forest

What is my passion?
Where is it hidden?
Where is my treasure?
Why can't I see it?

Wandering in the magical forest.
Magical trees there cover the sky.
Every tree is so endlessly bright.
I don't know which one I should climb.

Every tree reaches straight to the sky.
I am just a human with no power to fly.
And I am not able to climb every tree
In this magical forest that is hiding in me.

But all of them are so endlessly bright.
Beautiful, inspiring, gigantic, and quiet.
In order for me to reach up to the sky
I have to pick one, starting slowly to climb.

That is my passion!
There it is, hidden!
There is my treasure!
I can finally see it!

Reunion

Wet.
Our hands are wet.
We're both sweating.
We're both excited.
I can see her pupils.
They are getting wider.
I am covering her with my arms.
She is doing the same.
I can feel her breath on my neck.
My heartbeat is intensely high.
She feels the same.
I find her wrist and go down.
Finally, our hands are together again.
I can feel that her hand is wet.
Mine is wet too.
We don't care.
We never let them be apart again.
I am whispering, "I love you."
I can feel how she is pressing my hand.
She loves me too.
Not only are our hands wet.
We love crying because of happiness.
She looked at me and smiled.
How much I wanted to feel this again.
I love her eyes.

I know.
I am finally home.

Motherland

I was born in a country of violence.
Voices do nothing; we keep our silence.

What is the value of all broken dreams,
All sacrifices and thousands of tears?

Brothers and sisters are tired of fights.
Will someone ask you about your rights?

Our hands are in blood; theirs are clean.
And we ask our God: Why are You mean?

They are constantly breaking us down.
Somehow, we keep holding their crown.

717

God gave us self-awareness.
So He could laugh at us,
And we would understand the reasons why.

On My Way

People with masks on their faces.
Those are the same as the mask of my own.
Being in a crowd as a faceless unknown.
Feeling so sick, right down to the bone.
I am so tired of living alone.

People with smiles on their faces.
Those are the same as a smile of mine.
When facing life hardships, saying: "I'm fine."
And all of those tears I will try to confine.
Living in hope for a positive sign.

People with pains on their faces.
Those are the same as the pains I've felt.
When my heart is so cold and me being knelt.
Hands being tied to the walls with a belt.
Playing with cards that I've been dealt.

The train has stopped.
This is my station.
I need to get up.

Polaris

A small, little friend is burning at night.
Among other millions, he is so bright.
He is listening to me; he is looking at me;
He is making me feel like I can be free.

Under the tree, I like to sit on a whim,
Telling my worries, and my stories to him.
Incredible listener, an amazing advisor.
That helps me to be better and wiser.

I am raising my head and lifting my soul.
One on the planet, what is my role?
Among other millions, for what do I strive?
What does it mean to be staying alive?

You are, my friend, so far and so close;
You are the one I am telling the most.
Telling my worries, my stories, and dreams.
We are so similar, that's how it seems.

Numbers

There were trillions of atoms.
I love you so deeply and much,
With all of them in my body.

There were billions of stars.
You are brighter than them,
By more than a billion times.

There were millions of smiles.
And all they were all mine,
Just because of your one.

There were thousands of hugs.
And my stomach was full
with thousands of bugs.

There were hundreds of tears.
Mostly because of happiness,
And I will fight all of my fears.

There were dozens of people.
They all support our love,
Support both you and me.

And there was something unique.

It was your heart that found mine,
That showed the truth and love.

Four Seasons

1.
The beauty of snow.
The coldness of winter is warm.
Mesmerizing night.

2.
Flowers are blooming.
The silence of water is loud.
A small, shallow pond.

3.
The Moon is shining.
The stars are so bright tonight.
I can't fall asleep.

4.
Rain is falling down.
Tiny droplets hitting me -
Splashes of water.

That Cold, Rainy Morning

I remembered that cold, rainy Morning.
Outside it was lightning and storming.
I decided to open it and look at my phone.
Your Good Morning saying 'You aren't alone,'

I remembered those times when I was crying.
When my positivism was gradually dying.
And you came. You helped me at all times.
You built all of my poems and rhymes.

I appreciate and love you so much.
Please come and give me your touch.
A lot of my wishes, desires, and dreams:
Swimming with you in our live streams.

I am so happy to call you my Little Star.
I am proud of us; we have gotten so far.
You are my treasure, and you are my Sun.
You are my everything - we always have fun.

I want to remember that cold, rainy Morning.
When it is still raining and storming
I want to wake up and see your beautiful smile.
I want to cuddle you and hear your heart all
while.

I Am Here

Where are your friends?
Why are you sitting here alone?
Were you left behind?
Were you forgotten?
Was there no one waiting for you?
No one will ask how you are doing,
How your day is, or how your life's going.
Don't worry - there will always be
One person, at least.
I will be waiting for you.
I am ready to listen, and
I am willing to help.
No need to worry - there is support.
Just don't get upset. Stop looking down.
Please, stand up and take my hand.
Brighter days are waiting for you.
More people are waiting for you.
I am here, waiting for you.

Utopia

Ah, what a shitty world we live in:
Propaganda, delusions,
Ideologies, illusions,
The brutality of the "victims,"
And lies of the systems,
Substitution of concepts,
Censorship of the contents.
We forgot about the truth.
And we forgot about justice.
The stupidity of the youth,
And those who want to bust us.
Is there a remedy for society?
To return to the order and propriety?

Four Feelings

1.

An apple fell down
Directly on my shoulder.
There was once her head.

2.

Red enormous field.
Soldiers lying on the grass.
The bloody poppies.

3.

Tell me a story
About the old golden days.
Oh, a weird stranger.

4.

This trembling heart of mine.
When the mind is flying high,
Manifesting love.

The Fairy Greenhouse

The fairy greenhouse has opened its doors.
So much greenery it probably stores.
I am stepping inside and need to bend.
The smells are so bright, there's no end.

First of the flowers, I am tempted to see
Is the beautiful daisy that is looking at me.
Her treasure is innocence; her beauty is pure.
The smell of this flower has made me mature.

What is the next one I am going to see?
A red gladiolus resting near the tree.
Showing integrity and adamant strength.
Gracefully growing, demonstrating the length.

Continue walking through the greenery maze.
Where iris of blue has been smiling with grace.
Her present is faith, which will keep me upright.
Her present is hope, which will make me alright.

The tree of wisdom is so big and so strong.
I sat down under it to hear him singing a song.
The fairy greenhouse has opened its doors.
So much greenery it probably stores.

Rebellion

Soldiers of justice are committing a crime.
When thousands of people are ready to die,
For the sake of the future and our bright sky.
All of us are uniting: now is that time!

All lives matter; souls don't have colors!
We will be spreading the voices of love.
We will stop putting other people below.
We will all be calling each other brothers.

The candles of hope are burning inside.
I believe in humanity and the power of minds.
We will open those eyes - stop being blind!
The time has come to keep going and fight!

In The Morning

I was just a small, weak boy.
And you made me a strong, whole man.
And I felt it in my bones -
All this love
Was given just to me,
And I was glad to see
The way you looked at me.
Oh, this love.

Your soul is a chest of gold,
Your eyes are full of dreams.
Whenever I see them,
I see my future in.
Your heart is bumping fast,
I am lying on your chest.
The way you smiled at me
It felt like the sun and sea.

I was falling down.
You made me stay strong.
And I am keeping it now
All your love.
Being so far away
When hearts are very close.
That's what the feeling is

Having love.

And I am here with you,
I am holding both your hands.
I am hugging all of you.
I am feeling your hot breath.
Just remember all of this.
I will give you every kiss.
You are having all of me
With all my love.

It's You

Breaking borders and feeling new worlds,
You'll keep moving. There is no point in
stopping.
There is no point to lose. There's no point in
failing.
And you will keep moving.
With every new step, you will be closer and
closer.
Steps can be small, and steps can be large.
You will notice it without thought.
And you will be fighting with a goal in your
mind.
You will be crying without tears in your eyes.
Your heart's beating will be faster and faster.
You will be playing the game of life.
When rules are changing every second.
But you see your future, your "light in the end."
And your soul is calm now, your mind is clear.
The best music in your life will make your heart
beat like a drum.
It's you.

The Wildfire

Stupidity spreads like wildfire.
Burning individual trees,
And burning the whole forests.
Only small islands of wisdom
Can escape the rage of this fire.
Let knowledge spread,
And protect itself like the ocean.
To slow down the fires,
To spread wisdom like rain.

Brave Soldier

The brave soldier is fighting for you.
Keep your mind clean.
The brave soldier is dying for you.
Why are you always so mean?
The brave soldier is crying for you.
Where are your tears?
The brave soldier is protecting you.
Have you met your fears?
The brave soldier has died.
You are still here.
But who are you?
If no one remembers you.

Looking Up

Justice always wins the battle.
All good people will be crowned.
This world likes to see us crying,
But in response, we keep smiling.
Golden days are patiently waiting.
I will be there; no more hesitating.
One day, all of my sufferings will end.
We will be surrounded by many friends.
Black and white are always united.
With all of the colors, we are delighted.

We are All...

Ultimately, we are all lonely.

Ultimately, we are all kids.

Ultimately, we are all lost.

Ultimately, we are all here.

Ultimately, we are all searching.

Ultimately, we are all dreaming.

Ultimately, we are all wandering.

Ultimately, we are all living.

Reality

The truth is on our side;
It's sleeping now.
And the truth will arise
Like a Phoenix from the ashes.
And those who lie will burn in its fire.
Goodness is goodness, and evil is evil.

www.ingramcontent.com/pod-product-compliance
Lightning Source LLC
LaVergne TN
LVHW050506210726
843509LV00015BA/3016